INSIDE THE
NFL

TAMPA BAY
BUCCANEERS

BY ROBERT COOPER

SportsZone

An Imprint of Abdo Publishing
abdobooks.com

abdobooks.com

Published by Abdo Publishing, a division of ABDO, PO Box 398166, Minneapolis, Minnesota 55439. Copyright © 2020 by Abdo Consulting Group, Inc. International copyrights reserved in all countries. No part of this book may be reproduced in any form without written permission from the publisher. SportsZone™ is a trademark and logo of Abdo Publishing.

Printed in the United States of America, North Mankato, Minnesota
022019
092019

Cover Photo: Tom DiPace/AP Images
Interior Photos: Steve Nesius/AP Images, 4–5, 6, 29; Kevin Terrell/NFL Photos/AP Images, 9; NFL Photos/AP Images, 11; AP Images, 13, 15; Peter Read Miller/AP Images, 17; James Drake/Sports Illustrated/Getty Images, 19; Nate Fine/NFL/Getty Images Sport/Getty Images, 21; Sheehan/AP Images, 22; John Swart/AP Images, 25; Al Messerschmidt/AP Images, 27; Rusty Kennedy/AP Images, 31; Chris O'Meara/AP Images, 35, 39; Greg Trott/AP Images, 36, 43

Editor: Patrick Donnelly
Series Designer: Craig Hinton

Library of Congress Control Number: 2018965872

Publisher's Cataloging-in-Publication Data

Names: Cooper, Robert, author.
Title: Tampa Bay Buccaneers / by Robert Cooper
Description: Minneapolis, Minnesota : Abdo Publishing, 2020 | Series: Inside the NFL | Includes online resources and index.
Identifiers: ISBN 9781532118654 (lib. bdg.) | ISBN 9781532172830 (ebook)
Subjects: LCSH: Tampa Bay Buccaneers (Football team)--Juvenile literature. | National Football League--Juvenile literature. | Football teams--Juvenile literature. | American football--Juvenile literature.
Classification: DDC 796.33264--dc23

TABLE OF
CONTENTS

CHAPTER 1

FROM CHUMPS
TO CHAMPS

Getting to the Super Bowl took longer than anyone in the Tampa Bay Buccaneers organization expected. But in 2002, the Bucs assembled the right group of players and learned how to win on a consistent basis. The only thing that stood in the way of the team and professional football's biggest game was Veterans Stadium in Philadelphia.

Under coach Tony Dungy, the Bucs had become one of the top teams in the National Football League (NFL) during the late 1990s and early 2000s. But Veterans Stadium had proved to be a difficult place for the Buccaneers. In each of the previous two seasons, the Eagles had knocked Tampa Bay out of the National Football Conference (NFC) playoffs, both times at the Vet.

The Buccaneers' Warren Sapp kisses the Vince Lombardi Trophy after Tampa Bay won its first Super Bowl.

It cost Tampa Bay $8 million and four draft picks to acquire coach Jon Gruden from Oakland in 2002. But the deal paid off.

Dungy was the winningest head coach in Buccaneers history. He had guided the team to its best six-year period ever. But as the core players from those teams neared retirement, Tampa Bay's window of opportunity was closing. So Bucs owner Malcolm Glazer and his two sons fired Dungy after the 2001 season. Then, in an unusual move, the Buccaneers sent

$8 million and four draft picks to the Oakland Raiders for one of the hottest young head coaches in the NFL, Jon Gruden.

The Bucs did not get off to a great start under Gruden, as they lost their season opener to the New Orleans Saints. The team had a lot of veteran players, though, and quickly came together. Tampa Bay finished the 2002 regular season with a 12–4 record, the best in franchise history. It also won the NFC South and earned the second seed in the NFC playoffs.

However, Philadelphia owned home-field advantage throughout the NFC playoffs. In order to visit the Eagles for the third straight year, the Bucs first had to beat the San Francisco 49ers. Tampa Bay defended its home turf with a 31–6 win over San Francisco.

The Eagles came into the NFC Championship Game as four-point favorites over the Bucs. But despite the two previous playoff losses and a 20–10 loss in Philadelphia earlier that season, Gruden and the Buccaneers were confident.

COLD-WEATHER GAMES

In their first 27 seasons, the Buccaneers, coming from warm and sunny Florida, did not win a game in which the temperature at the stadium was below 40 degrees Fahrenheit (4°C) at kickoff. Jon Gruden's team broke that streak with a 15–0 win in Chicago in the final game of the regular season on December 29, 2002.

The Vet was set to be demolished after the game to make way for a new stadium. But first the Buccaneers intended to demolish Philadelphia's Super Bowl aspirations.

That's exactly what they did. Thanks to their bruising defense, the Bucs' more mediocre offense didn't need to score a ton of points. Sometimes the defense helped there, too. Late in the fourth quarter, cornerback Ronde Barber returned an interception 92 yards for a touchdown. That play secured Tampa Bay's 27–10 win over Philadelphia and sent the Bucs to their first Super Bowl.

In order to come home with the Lombardi Trophy, Gruden and the Buccaneers would have to defeat his former team. Behind quarterback Rich Gannon—the league's Most Valuable Player (MVP) that season—the Oakland Raiders had won the American Football Conference (AFC) to qualify for Super Bowl XXXVII on January 26, 2003, in San Diego.

It wasn't even close. Tampa Bay made history in its 48–21 victory, intercepting Gannon a record five times and returning three for touchdowns. Buccaneers safety Dexter Jackson had two of the interceptions and was named the game's MVP. Dwight Smith also had two interceptions. He returned both for touchdowns in the second half.

✗ Dexter Jackson heads upfield after his second interception of Super Bowl XXXVII.

In addition, Tampa Bay sacked Gannon five times. Bucs quarterback Brad Johnson threw two touchdown passes to Keenan McCardell, while running back Michael Pittman rushed for 124 yards. It was a dominating performance.

Florida is often referred to as the "Sunshine State." The NFL awarded Tampa Bay a franchise on April 24, 1974. It took 27 seasons for the sun to shine on Tampa Bay in the form of a Vince Lombardi Trophy. But for Bucs fans, it was worth the wait.

CHAPTER 2

THE YUCKS

The Tampa Bay area is known for beaches. But the city of Tampa wanted a pro football team as well. A committee was formed in the Tampa Bay area in 1968 in hopes of landing an NFL team. Hope became a reality when the NFL decided to expand, awarding the twenty-seventh and twenty-eighth teams to Tampa and Seattle, Washington, respectively.

Hugh Culverhouse was an attorney and real estate investor in Jacksonville, Florida. Culverhouse had previously declined ownership of the Seattle team because it would play thousands of miles from where he lived. So when the opportunity arose to own a new team in Florida, he jumped at it. Culverhouse was awarded the Tampa Bay franchise on December 5, 1974. The two expansion teams were set to begin play in 1976.

Center Dan Ryczek stands in the huddle during Tampa Bay's 13–10 loss to Seattle in 1976. The Bucs went 0–14 in their first season.

Culverhouse did not want to relocate to the West Coast to own the Seahawks. But that did not stop him from visiting the West. In fact, he made the long trip to California many times with the goal of recruiting Tampa Bay's first head coach.

Culverhouse wanted to hire John McKay. He had impressive credentials. McKay had won four national championships with the University of Southern California. On October 31, 1975, McKay accepted the offer to become the first coach of the Buccaneers.

New teams are usually considered a work in progress. So expecting more losses than wins was realistic for Bucs fans in the team's first season. But was it too much to hope for a single win? Apparently so.

Any lofty expectations were quickly tempered when the Buccaneers lost their first two games by a combined score

✕ Quarterback Steve Spurrier goes down in a pile of Kansas City Chiefs defenders in Tampa Bay's 28–19 loss in October 1976.

of 43–0. In fact, in their inaugural season, which consisted of 14 games, the Bucs were shut out five times.

Tampa Bay's defense was not much better. As a result, the Bucs became the first NFL team to ever go 0–14 in a regular season. They were the lone winless team of the Super Bowl era (post-1966) until the 2008 Detroit Lions and 2017 Cleveland Browns (who both went 0–16) suffered the same fate.

TAMPA STADIUM

The original Tampa Stadium was dedicated on November 4, 1967. The University of Tennessee defeated the University of Tampa 38–0 in the first game at the stadium, which cost $4.1 million to build. Its original capacity of 46,700 was later expanded to 72,000. Tampa Stadium was demolished in 1998 when the Buccaneers moved into a new stadium.

The 1977 season was not much better. Tampa Bay was shut out six times that year. Of course, this did not sit well with McKay. But his quick wit and sense of humor helped pull his team through the tough times. For example, when he once was asked what he thought of the offense's execution, McKay jokingly replied, "I'm in favor of it."

Tampa Bay's offense ranked dead last in 1976 and 1977. The defense, however, was respectable, finishing in the middle of the pack in the team's second year. It also played a key role in helping the Bucs secure their first regular-season win. Tampa Bay scored three defensive touchdowns in a 33–14 victory over the Saints in New Orleans on December 11, 1977. The Bucs followed that upset with a 17–7 win at home over the St. Louis Cardinals the next week.

✕ Linebacker Richard Wood celebrates after Tampa Bay earned its first win, 33–14, at New Orleans on December 11, 1977.

Tampa Bay finished the 1977 season 2–12. The 2–26 start was the worst two-year stretch in NFL history until the 2016 and 2017 Cleveland Browns managed to do worse at 1–31. But the Bucs' 0–26 start remains the league's longest losing streak since the 1940s.

CHAPTER 3

FROM WORST TO FIRST

Tampa Bay continued to show some improvement the next year. The team boosted its record from 2–12 in 1977 to 5–11 in 1978. Finally, after combining for just seven wins in their first three seasons, the John McKay–led Buccaneers turned a corner in 1979.

The Bucs benefitted from the emergence of some key offensive players. Two of them were running back Ricky Bell and quarterback Doug Williams. Bell was a first-round draft pick in 1977. Williams was a first-round choice in 1978. The team's improved offensive line also surrendered only 12 sacks in 1979 after allowing 52 the previous season.

The defense carried its share of the load, too. Defensive end Lee Roy Selmon came into his own as the leader of the

Defensive end Lee Roy Selmon played a key role in Tampa Bay's breakthrough.

Tampa Bay's first three seasons were mostly forgettable. But the national media took notice of the Buccaneers after their surprising 5–0 start in 1979. In fact, Dewey Selmon—Lee Roy's brother—graced the *Sports Illustrated* cover that read, "Tampa Bay: Unbeaten, Untied and Unbelievable." Dewey was a defensive tackle/linebacker for the team. He was pictured tackling a Los Angeles Rams player.

defense in 1979. The fourth-year pro out of the University of Oklahoma led the team with 11 sacks and was named the NFL Defensive Player of the Year. Meanwhile, Tampa Bay's defense allowed the fewest points and yards in the NFL that season.

With their balanced attack, the Buccaneers shocked the world. They got off to a 5–0 start in 1979. While the defense led the way, the offense carried its weight. It scored 17 or more points in each of those wins. That included a 31–16 victory over the Detroit Lions to start the season.

Tampa Bay rode that start all the way to a 10–6 record and its first NFC Central title and playoff appearance. In the postseason, the Cinderella story continued. The Bucs defeated the visiting Philadelphia Eagles 24–17 in the divisional round, leaving them just one win away from going to the Super Bowl. This was difficult for anyone to believe, especially NFL experts outside the Tampa Bay area.

The Rams wrap up Buccaneers running back Ricky Bell in the NFC Championship Game on January 6, 1980. Los Angeles won 9–0.

The underdog Bucs hosted the Los Angeles Rams in the NFC Championship Game on January 6, 1980. Unfortunately for the Bucs, the offensive woes of the past emerged again. Tampa Bay lost 9–0 to Los Angeles. The Rams advanced to Super Bowl XIV.

CHAPTER 4

BACK TO
THE BOTTOM

The Buccaneers went 5–10–1 in 1980. But they bounced back in 1981 by compiling a 9–7 record, good enough for their second NFC Central division title in three years. The team then posted a 5–4 record in a strike-shortened season en route to another playoff appearance in 1982.

However, those trips to the playoffs did not prove to be as fruitful as the first for Tampa Bay. The Dallas Cowboys hosted—and defeated—the Bucs in the playoffs in consecutive seasons by a combined score of 68–17.

It appeared that Tampa Bay's window of opportunity had closed. As a result, many changes occurred. The Bucs team that coach John McKay had built was slowly dismantled.

Bucs quarterback Doug Williams directs traffic as he looks for running room.

× Tampa Bay wide receiver Gerald Carter takes a tumble against Detroit in 1983. The 1980s were difficult years for the Bucs.

After Tampa Bay's second postseason loss to Dallas, the team had an off-field issue. Bucs owner Hugh Culverhouse and the team's quarterback, Doug Williams, engaged in an ugly contract dispute. It resulted in Williams leaving the NFL for the United States Football League (USFL).

The USFL started play in 1983. It was created to compete with the NFL. The USFL lasted only three seasons, however. Williams eventually returned to the NFL to play with Washington.

In 1983 the Bucs struggled to recover from the loss of Williams. As a result, Tampa Bay started that season 0–9. The Bucs finished 2–14. It was their worst record since 1977.

James Wilder was the team's lone bright spot the next couple of years. He rushed for 1,544 yards and 13 touchdowns in 1984. Wilder carried the ball 407 times, an NFL record at the time. He followed that Pro Bowl season with another strong year in 1985, when he rushed for 1,300 yards and 10 touchdowns.

But rebuilding the Buccaneers would be a big challenge. McKay showed little interest in that task. Tampa Bay defeated the New York Jets 41–21 on December 16, 1984, giving the Bucs

BO SAYS NO

Running back Bo Jackson won the 1985 Heisman Trophy at Auburn University. He was also a star baseball player. So when he learned the Bucs might select him with the first overall pick in the 1986 NFL Draft, he said he'd rather play pro baseball. Still, the Bucs picked Jackson, who bailed on Tampa Bay and played baseball for the Kansas City Royals instead. Jackson went back into the NFL Draft the next year and was picked by the Los Angeles Raiders. He established himself as one of the league's best backs with them. He continued to play for the Royals during the baseball season.

LEE ROY SELMON

Bucs defensive end Lee Roy Selmon played in his final Pro Bowl on January 27, 1985. It turned out to be his last football game. Selmon missed the entire 1985 season because of a herniated disc in his neck. The injury forced him to retire. The six-time Pro Bowl selection holds the franchise's unofficial all-time sack record with 78.5. (The NFL did not track sacks as an official statistic until 1982.) On July 29, 1995, he became the first Buccaneer inducted into the Pro Football Hall of Fame.

a 6–10 record to finish the season. It turned out to be McKay's last game in Tampa Bay. His resignation set off a coaching carousel that seemed destined to never stop.

McKay finished his time as Buccaneers coach with an overall regular-season record of 44–88–1. The Bucs hired former Atlanta Falcons head coach Leeman Bennett as McKay's replacement. It did not take long for Culverhouse to determine that Bennett was not the man for the job. Bennett was fired after posting consecutive 2–14 seasons in 1985 and 1986.

Former University of Alabama head coach Ray Perkins was up next. He won just 19 regular-season games in four years with the Bucs and was fired late in the 1990 season. Interim head coach Richard Williamson was retained for 1991. But he was let go at the end of that season after the Bucs went 3–13.

✗ Chicago Bears defensive end Richard Dent sacks Tampa Bay quarterback Vinny Testaverde in 1988.

It was clear that Culverhouse needed a proven head coach who commanded respect. In 1992 he hired Sam Wyche, who had led the Cincinnati Bengals to the Super Bowl just a few years earlier. But the losing atmosphere remained in Tampa Bay, where Wyche guided the team to just 23 victories in four seasons.

The Bucs had once again become the laughingstock of the NFL. They suffered through 14 straight losing seasons under five different head coaches.

CHAPTER 5

BUILDING A CONTENDER

On August 25, 1994, Buccaneers owner Hugh Culverhouse died. He had been the Bucs' only owner in their almost 20 years of existence. Less than six months later, Malcolm Glazer—an investor from West Palm Beach, Florida— purchased the team for $192 million. The Glazer family had aggressive plans. Those plans started with a new look and new stadium for the team.

The next order of business was finding a new head coach. The Glazers and general manager Rich McKay embarked on a long coaching search. McKay was the son of former Bucs coach John McKay. They hired Tony Dungy on January 22, 1996. Dungy had previously served as a successful defensive coordinator for the Minnesota Vikings.

Head Coach Tony Dungy led Tampa Bay to a period of success in the late 1990s and early 2000s.

The Bucs got off to a 1–8 start under Dungy, but they stuck together. Their young roster had promise. The players were buying into Dungy's calm demeanor and soft-spoken message. The Buccaneers won five of their final seven games to finish the 1996 season 6–10.

The Bucs entered 1997 with new uniforms of red and pewter (a silver-gray color) and a skull-and-crossed-swords battle-flag logo. Team leaders emerged, such as fullback Mike Alstott, linebacker Derrick Brooks, safety John Lynch, linebacker Hardy Nickerson, and defensive tackle Warren Sapp. Rookie running back Warrick Dunn rushed for 978 yards and made the Pro Bowl. The Bucs stunned the NFL by starting out 5–0.

The fast beginning led to a strong 1997 season. Tampa Bay finished 10–6 and made the playoffs for the first time since 1982. The Bucs capped off that memorable season with a 20–10 home win over

TAMPA 2

Tampa Bay earned a reputation for strong defense in the late 1990s. The Bucs ranked in the top three in total defense from 1997 to 1999. They frequently used a Cover 2 defensive system. The scheme uses two safeties to cover the deep zones away from the ball, with cornerbacks and linebackers covering the rest. With fast athletes, it can be effective. The Bucs played it so well that it came to be known as the "Tampa 2."

Tampa Bay defenders swarm Detroit punter John Jett during the Buccaneers' 20–10 wild-card playoff win on December 28, 1997.

Detroit in the playoffs. But they were eliminated by host Green Bay the next week.

Three playoff appearances in Dungy's first five seasons on the job sent a message to the rest of the NFL: The Bucs had turned a corner. In 1999 the Bucs had their best season ever at the time, posting an 11–5 record. They also won the NFC Central, their first divisional title in 18 years. The Bucs' defense ranked third in the NFL.

The Buccaneers won a thrilling 14–13 home playoff game over the Washington Redskins. The next week, they traveled to St. Louis for an NFC Championship Game showdown with the Rams. St. Louis had the NFL's top scoring offense that season. The Bucs played well, especially on defense. They nearly pulled off the upset. But the Rams survived with an 11–6 victory.

Under Dungy, the Bucs had washed away the stench of losing. They established themselves as a legitimate playoff contender. Expectations were extremely high. The team's ownership group, the Glazer family, hungered for Tampa Bay to win a Super Bowl.

RAYMOND JAMES STADIUM

The Bucs played their last game at their old stadium in 1997. Their new facility, Raymond James Stadium, opened in September 1998. It is known around the NFL for its unique 103-foot (31 m) pirate ship.

The Glazers had invested a lot of money in free-agent contracts for quarterback Brad Johnson and defensive end Simeon Rice. They had also traded for standout wide receiver Keyshawn Johnson and made other signings designed to improve the roster.

Tampa Bay's loss to the Rams in the NFC Championship Game after the 1999 season still stung

✗ Wide receiver Keyshawn Johnson was a controversial figure in his short time with the Buccaneers.

the Glazers. The family believed the team's window of opportunity for a Super Bowl might be closing. A 10–6 season in 2000 ended with a 21–3 loss to Philadelphia in the playoffs. That postseason defeat put Dungy's job status in question heading into the 2001 season.

The Bucs did not deliver. The team produced a 9–7 record and barely made the playoffs. With Dungy's job reportedly on the line heading into the team's first-round postseason game, the players did not respond. The result was an ugly 31–9 loss and a second straight playoff exit in Philadelphia.

On January 14, 2002, the Glazers fired Dungy. At the time, he was Tampa Bay's all-time winningest head coach. He left Tampa Bay with a regular-season record of 54–42 and four playoff appearances.

Ownership's original plan was to lure Bill Parcells out of retirement. Parcells was a two-time Super Bowl winner with the New York Giants. But at the last minute, he decided to remain retired. The Glazers had no backup plan. Fans were becoming impatient. But ownership worked to pull off a major, and unusual, trade. The Bucs acquired Jon Gruden from the Oakland Raiders on February 20, 2002.

It is almost unheard of for a team to trade for a coach. Not only did the Glazers negotiate the deal with Raiders owner Al Davis, the Buccaneers also paid a king's ransom. Tampa Bay sent Oakland $8 million, two first-round draft picks, and two second-round draft selections in exchange for the NFL's youngest head coach.

Gruden was 38 years old at the time of the trade. He had already established himself as one of the NFL's brightest offensive minds in four seasons as coach of the Raiders. Filling Dungy's shoes was not going to be easy. But Gruden understood the expectations: Super Bowl or bust.

So he revamped Tampa Bay's underachieving offense and challenged the defense to dominate in 2002, which it did. The end result was a division title, a team-best 12–4 record, and playoff wins over San Francisco and Philadelphia. The dream season was capped off with the 48–21 Super Bowl win over Oakland, making the trade for Gruden worth every penny and draft pick.

CHAPTER 6

BACK ON THE COACHING CAROUSEL

The Bucs' momentum as Super Bowl champions unofficially ended in a 38–35 overtime loss to the Indianapolis Colts on October 6, 2003. Tampa Bay blew a 35–14 lead with four minutes remaining. This allowed the Colts, led by former Bucs head coach Tony Dungy, to pull off one of the biggest come-from-behind wins in NFL history.

The confetti had stopped falling at that point, and the Bucs' unraveling began. In November 2003, head coach Jon Gruden had a falling out with Rich McKay and star receiver Keyshawn Johnson. McKay, the general manager, left Tampa Bay to join the division rival Atlanta Falcons.

Indianapolis's Raheem Brock trips up Tampa Bay's Mike Alstott during the Colts' amazing comeback victory.

✕ Linebacker Derrick Brooks was an 11-time Pro Bowl pick during his 14-year career in Tampa Bay.

Johnson was taken off the team's active roster, and eventually he was traded to Dallas.

McKay was replaced by Bruce Allen. He had worked with Gruden in Oakland. Allen inherited a financial mess with the Bucs. Long, expensive contracts had been awarded to too many players. Tampa Bay went 7–9 in 2003. Before the next season, Allen decided to cut expenses by parting ways with aging fan favorites such as safety John Lynch and defensive tackle Warren Sapp.

Despite having so much roster turnover, Gruden managed to lead the Buccaneers to two more NFC South division titles in 2005 and 2007. However, Tampa Bay failed to win another playoff game after its Super Bowl run. Gruden and Allen were fired in January 2009. Gruden finished his time in Tampa Bay as the winningest head coach in Bucs history. He left town with a regular-season record of 57–55.

Gruden's record looked good in comparison to men who led the Buccaneers in the following 10 seasons. From 2009 to 2016, the Bucs changed coaches four times. They had two winning seasons. And they made zero playoff appearances.

Raheem Morris was promoted from defensive coordinator to replace Gruden. He was the youngest coach in the NFL at 32. But with a young head coach and a rookie quarterback in Josh Freeman, the Bucs finished just 3–13 in 2009. They rebounded the next year to go 10–6, and fans started to get excited about Freeman being a

A-TRAIN'S LAST STOP

Fullback Mike Alstott's bruising running style earned him the nickname "A-Train." In the summer of 2007, Alstott suffered his second neck injury in less than five years. This led to his retirement after 11 seasons. Through 2018, Alstott was Tampa Bay's second-leading rusher (5,088 yards) and all-time touchdown leader (71).

FRESH LOOK, FRESH START

The 1997 Buccaneers donned new uniforms that helped them shed the ugliness of the "Yucks" era. The Bucs hoped for a similar jumpstart from a uniform overhaul after the 2013 season. The uniforms kept the pewter and red but added back in some orange from the original Bucs color scheme.

potential franchise quarterback. He threw 25 touchdown passes and only six interceptions that season. Only a tiebreaker kept the Buccaneers out of the playoffs.

Morris was fired after the Bucs fell to 4–12 in 2011. Up next was Greg Schiano, a longtime college coach who had spent the previous 11 years at Rutgers University. Schiano tried to bring some of his college ways to the NFL. One attempt to turn the team around was a code of discipline he called "the Buccaneer Way." It was a new attitude for Tampa Bay football.

But the results did not improve. Freeman's play declined and he was benched. Rookie running back Doug Martin was one of the team's few bright spots in 2012. Martin rushed for 1,454 yards and 11 touchdowns that year. However, after winning just 11 games in two years, Schiano was gone.

The Bucs tried a coach with more NFL experience next. Lovie Smith had been the Tampa Bay linebackers coach in the 1990s. He went on to lead the Chicago Bears to the Super Bowl

The Buccaneers made Florida State quarterback Jameis Winston the top pick in the 2015 NFL Draft.

after the 2006 season. He was hired as Tampa Bay's head coach in 2014.

After going 2–14 in Smith's first year, the Bucs earned the No. 1 draft pick. They used it to select quarterback Jameis Winston. Winston was a Heisman Trophy winner from nearby

MIKE EVANS

Receiver Mike Evans rocketed up the Tampa Bay leaderboards after entering the league in 2014. In 2018 he passed Jimmie Giles for most touchdown receptions in franchise history with 35. He was one of only three players in NFL history to record 1,000 or more receiving yards in each of his first four seasons.

Florida State University. Bucs fans hoped they finally had a franchise quarterback.

Winston started every game his rookie year. Despite some growing pains, he performed well enough to be selected to the Pro Bowl. And Martin had a comeback season, rushing for more than 1,400 yards and making his second Pro Bowl. The Bucs finished fifth in the NFL in total yards. But they finished with a 6–10 record. Smith was fired after the season.

Next in line was offensive coordinator Dirk Koetter, who was promoted to head coach. He was responsible for the team's offense in 2015. Another weapon that had emerged for the Bucs was wide receiver Mike Evans. A first-round draft pick in 2014, Evans started his career with five consecutive 1,000-yard receiving seasons. The Buccaneers went 9–7 in Koetter's first year. It was their first winning record since 2010. Winston improved slightly, as did Evans. But like 2010, they missed the playoffs on a tiebreaker. After a disappointing 5–11 season

FITZMAGIC

In 2018 the Bucs appeared to be in trouble with starting quarterback Jameis Winston suspended for the first three games. Ryan Fitzpatrick was the team's backup. Fitzpatrick was in his 14th year in the league. He had mostly been a backup. Not much was expected of him. But instead, Fitzpatrick dominated. He threw for 400 yards in each of the team's first three games. That had never been done in NFL history. The Bucs started 2–1. But the "Fitzmagic" ran out in Week 4. The Bucs lost at Chicago, and Winston was restored as the starter the next week.

in 2017, the team had gone 10 straight seasons without a playoff appearance.

Winston showed in 2017 he could be an elite quarterback. He threw a career-low 11 interceptions. He had his best passer rating ever. The Bucs hoped he would be even better in 2018. But Winston was suspended for an off-field incident to start the season. Backup Ryan Fitzpatrick had to play, and he got the team off to a fast start. Winston regained the job, but his inconsistent play was a factor in the team's 5–11 record. Koetter was fired at the end of the season and replaced by former Arizona Cardinals head coach Bruce Arians. In five seasons with the Cardinals, Arians averaged almost 10 wins per season. The Buccaneers are hoping he can bring that track record of success with him to Tampa Bay.

TIMELINE

1974
Hugh Culverhouse is awarded the Tampa Bay franchise.

1975
John McKay leaves his college post with Southern California to become Tampa Bay's first head coach on October 31.

1977
The Bucs earn the franchise's first regular-season victory and end a 26-game losing streak with a 33–14 defeat of the New Orleans Saints on December 11.

1979
The Bucs clinch their first NFC Central Division championship and playoff berth.

1980
One week after winning its first playoff game, Tampa Bay loses to the Los Angeles Rams 9–0 on January 6 in its first appearance in an NFC Championship Game.

1984
After three trips to the playoffs from 1979 to 1983, McKay resigns as Tampa Bay's coach.

1994
On August 25, Culverhouse dies. The team is placed in the control of a three-man trust led by Culverhouse's law partner, Steven Story.

1995
West Palm Beach investor Malcolm Glazer purchases the Buccaneers on January 16 for $192 million.

1995
On July 29, Lee Roy Selmon becomes the first player in the history of the team to be inducted into the Pro Football Hall of Fame.

1997
The Bucs make their first playoff appearance since 1982 and win their first playoff game in 18 years with a 20–10 home victory over the Detroit Lions on December 28.

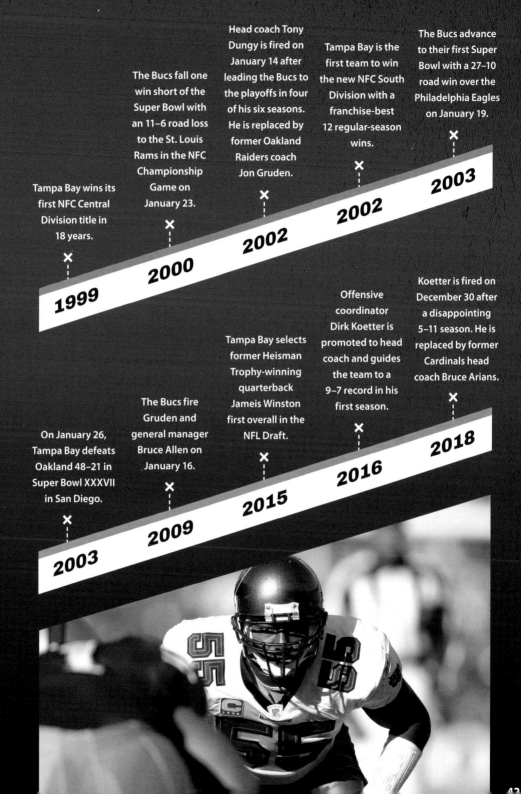

Tampa Bay wins its first NFC Central Division title in 18 years.

The Bucs fall one win short of the Super Bowl with an 11–6 road loss to the St. Louis Rams in the NFC Championship Game on January 23.

Head coach Tony Dungy is fired on January 14 after leading the Bucs to the playoffs in four of his six seasons. He is replaced by former Oakland Raiders coach Jon Gruden.

Tampa Bay is the first team to win the new NFC South Division with a franchise-best 12 regular-season wins.

The Bucs advance to their first Super Bowl with a 27–10 road win over the Philadelphia Eagles on January 19.

1999
2000
2002
2002
2003

On January 26, Tampa Bay defeats Oakland 48–21 in Super Bowl XXXVII in San Diego.

The Bucs fire Gruden and general manager Bruce Allen on January 16.

Tampa Bay selects former Heisman Trophy-winning quarterback Jameis Winston first overall in the NFL Draft.

Offensive coordinator Dirk Koetter is promoted to head coach and guides the team to a 9–7 record in his first season.

Koetter is fired on December 30 after a disappointing 5–11 season. He is replaced by former Cardinals head coach Bruce Arians.

2003
2009
2015
2016
2018

QUICK STATS

FRANCHISE HISTORY

1976–

SUPER BOWLS
(*wins in bold*)

2002 (XXXVII)

NFC CHAMPIONSHIP GAMES

1979, 1999, 2002

DIVISION CHAMPIONSHIPS

1979, 1981, 1999, 2002, 2005, 2007

KEY COACHES

Tony Dungy (1996–2001): 54–42,
2–4 (playoffs)
Jon Gruden (2002–2008): 57–55,
3–2 (playoffs)
John McKay (1976–84): 44–88–1,
1–3 (playoffs)

KEY PLAYERS *(positions, seasons with team)*

Mike Alstott (FB, 1996–2006)
Ronde Barber (CB, 1997–2012)
Derrick Brooks (LB, 1995–2008)
Jimmie Giles (TE, 1978–86)
Paul Gruber (OT, 1988–99)
John Lynch (S, 1993–2003)
Gerald McCoy (DT, 2010–)
Hardy Nickerson (LB, 1993–99)
Shelton Quarles (LB, 1997–2006)
Simeon Rice (DE, 2001–06)
Warren Sapp (DT, 1995–2003)
Lee Roy Selmon (DE, 1976–84)
James Wilder (FB/RB, 1981–89)
Doug Williams (QB, 1978–82)
Jameis Winston (QB, 2015–)

HOME FIELDS

Raymond James Stadium (1998–)
Tampa Stadium (1976–97)
   Also known as
      Houlihan's Stadium

*All statistics through 2018 season

QUOTES AND ANECDOTES

"For me, this is hard to put in perspective. But we've got something bigger yet to accomplish. We're on a path of destiny, and we don't want to mess that up now."

—Buccaneers cornerback Ronde Barber, after helping the team defeat the Eagles in the NFC Championship Game in January 2003

"There was no penalty on the play, so Doug must have bit himself in the lip and broke his jaw."

—Bucs coach John McKay, when asked how quarterback Doug Williams suffered a broken jaw after a late hit against the Rams in 1978

"The way they stocked the teams [through the veteran allocation process] just wasn't a fair way to do it. People in L. A. thought I was off my rocker to take the Tampa Bay job. I saw the chance to build something that would last. Maybe I was a little naive. In looking back, I did not know exactly what was entailed in this situation. I don't believe it was conducive to winning."

—John McKay, the Bucs' first coach, on the task of building an expansion team into winners

The Tony Dungy era ended in Tampa Bay without a championship. But the coach remained a legendary figure among Bucs fans. In 2018 Dungy became the twelfth person inducted into the Buccaneers' Ring of Honor. He was honored at halftime of a Week 3 game against the Pittsburgh Steelers.

GLOSSARY

contender
A person or team that has a good chance at winning a championship.

contract
An agreement to play for a certain team.

coordinator
An assistant coach who is in charge of the offense or defense.

draft
A system that allows teams to acquire new players coming into a league.

expansion
The addition of new teams to increase the size of a league.

franchise
A sports organization, including the top-level team and all minor league affiliates.

Heisman Trophy
The award given yearly to the best player in college football.

interception
A pass intended for an offensive player that is caught by a defensive player.

interim
Temporary.

passer rating
A statistic that measures a quarterback's overall effectiveness.

rookie
A professional athlete in his or her first year of competition.

sack
A tackle of the quarterback behind the line of scrimmage before he can pass the ball.

MORE INFORMATION

BOOKS

Karras, Steven M. *Tampa Bay Buccaneers*. New York: AV2 by Weigl, 2018.

Kortemeier, Todd. *Tampa Bay Buccaneers*. Minneapolis, MN: Abdo Publishing, 2017.

Lajiness, Katie. *Tampa Bay Buccaneers*. Minneapolis, MN: Abdo Publishing, 2017.

ONLINE RESOURCES

Booklinks
NONFICTION NETWORK
FREE! ONLINE NONFICTION RESOURCES

To learn more about the Tampa Bay Buccaneers, visit **abdobooklinks.com** or scan this QR code. These links are routinely monitored and updated to provide the most current information available.

PLACE TO VISIT

Pro Football Hall of Fame
2121 George Halas Dr. NW
Canton, OH 44708
330–456–8207
profootballhof.com

This hall of fame and museum highlights the greatest players and moments in the history of the National Football League. Eight people affiliated with the Buccaneers are enshrined, including defensive linemen Lee Roy Selmon and Warren Sapp and coach Tony Dungy.

INDEX

ABOUT THE AUTHOR

Robert Cooper is a retired law enforcement officer and lifelong NFL fan. He and his wife live in Seattle near their only son and two grandchildren.